The Campfire Songs Pocketbook

This book is comprised of the many campfire
songs that are not copyrighted and can be found
in many versions in a variety of formats.
Although this book as a whole is copyrighted, no
claim to any song copyright is claimed.

First Edition

First Printing, 2014

ISBN 978-1-291-87323-8

D1808209

Front cover image courtesy of Wikipedia

Contents

Campfires Burning

(To the tune of London's burning)

Camp fire's Burning, Camp fire's burning
Draw nearer, Draw nearer
In the gloaming, in the gloaming
Come sing and be merry...

Continue in a round if desired or just repeat
through a few times getting louder.

Use this song as a way of warming everyone up
to get them in a singing mood, so getting them
to sing louder and competing is a good start.

Fast Food

(To the tune of a ram sam sam)
This is an action song and the actions are at the end

A Pizza Hut a Pizza Hut
Kentucky Fried Chicken and a Pizza Hut
A Pizza Hut a Pizza Hut
Kentucky Fried Chicken and a Pizza Hut
McDonald McDonalds
Kentucky Fried Chicken and a Pizza Hut

Pizza Hut - Make shape of a hut in the air.
Kentucky Fried Chicken - Flap arms like a chicken.
McDonalds – Use hands above your head to make the McDonalds 'M'.

Ging Gang Gooli

Ging gang gooli gooli gooli gooli watcha, ging
gang goo, ging gang goo. [Repeat.]
Heyla, oh heyla sheyla, oh heyla sheyla heyla
hoo. [Repeat.]
Shala walli, shala walli, shala walli, shala walli,
Oompha, Oompah . . .

Sing as a round, with one group continuing with
the 'Oompah' and another singing the song
again from the beginning; then switch.

If you are really adventurous try several groups
only one or two lines behind each other.

He Jumped Without a Parachute

He jumped without a parachute from forty
thousand feet
He jumped without a parachute from forty
thousand feet
He jumped without a parachute from forty
thousand feet
And he 'aint gonna jump no more

Chorus
Glory, glory what a hell of a way to die
Glory, glory what a hell of a way to die
Glory, glory what a hell of a way to die
And he 'aint gonna jump no more

He landed on the tarmac like a lump of
strawberry jam (3x)
Chorus

They put him in a matchbox and they sent him
home to mum (3x)
Chorus

She put him on the mantel piece for everyone to
see (3x)
Chorus

He fell in to the fire and was never seen again
(3x) (Sung with sadness)

Last Chorus

Alice the Camel

Alice the camel has 10 humps, Alice the camel
has 10 humps
Alice the camel has 10 humps, so go, Alice,
GO!!

(Continue with 9, 8, 7 . . . humps, until . . .)

Alice the camel has no humps, Alice the camel
has no humps
Alice the camel has no humps, 'cause Alice is a
HORSE!!

Bingo Was His Name-o

There was a farmer had a dog and Bingo was his name-o'
B-I-N-G-O, B-I-N-G-O, B-I-N-G-O, and Bingo was his name-o.

Sing song through six times, the first time just spelling out
the name BINGO; second time, clap the 'B' and spell out the last four letters; third time, clap the 'B' and the 'I' and so on until all five letters are clapped
out.

Baby Bumblebee

I caught a little baby bumblebee,
Won't my Mummy be surprised at me,
I caught a little baby bumblebee,
(Spoken) Ow!, he stung me!

I squashed a little baby bumblebee,
Won't my Mummy be surprised at me…
(Spoken) Eurgh, my hands are sticky!

I'm licking off a baby bumblebee,
Won't my Mummy be surprised at me…
(Spoken) Oh, I feel sick!

I'm sicking up a baby bumblebee,
Won't my Mummy be surprised at me…
(Spoken) Oh, the floor is all messy!

I'm sweeping up a baby bumblebee,
Won't my Mummy be surprised at me…

Father Abraham

Father Abraham had seven sons,
Seven sons had Father Abraham.
And they never laughed, and they never cried,
All the did was go like this:
(Swing left arm round)

Repeat and add on the following actions each time:
Swing right arm round
Circle left leg
Circle right leg
Nod
Wiggle bottom.

Head, Shoulders, Knees and Toes

Head and shoulders, knees and toes, knees and toes.
Head and shoulders, knees and toes, knees and toes.
Eye and ears, and a mouth and a nose.
Head and shoulders, knees and toes, knees and toes.

Touch the appropriate body part each time it's mentioned.
Second time round: don't say the word 'head' aloud, but still touch it.
Each verse thereafter, don't say the next body part but still touch it until the entire song is no longer sung but just actioned.

Singing in the Rain

I'm singing in the rain, just singing in the rain.
What a glorious feeling, I'm happy again.
Thumbs up! [Group echoes.]
A choo cha cha, a choo cha cha, a choo cha cha
cha [Group joins in]

Add each of the following, in turn:
Elbows in
Knees bent
Toes together
Bums out
Chest out
Chin down
Tongue out

The Little Green Frog

Um-ah [with the tongue], went the little green
frog one day.
Um-ah, went the little green frog.
Um-ah, went the little green frog one day.
And the frog he went um-ah, um-ah, ah.

Repeat getting faster each time until group can
no longer copy.

Over the Irish Sea

When I was one, I had just begun, the day I went
to sea
I climbed aboard a pirate ship and the captain
said to me,
We'll go this way, that way, forward and back,
over the Irish Sea, (with actions jumping left,
right, forward, backward)
A bottle of rum to soothe my tum,
And that's the life for me.
Da, da, da, dum; da, da, da, dum . . .

When I was two, I tied my shoe . . .
When I was three, I bumped my knee . . .
When I was four, I shut the door . . .
When I was five, I was still alive . . .
When I was six, I gathered sticks . . .
When I was seven, I was almost in heaven . . .
When I was eight, I closed the gate . . .
When I was nine, I was feeling fine . . .
When I was ten, I started again . . .

Other actions:
Climbed aboard... – Climb up the rope ladder
The captain said... – Give a salute
Over the Irish Sea... - Make waves with hand
Bottle of rum... – Lift up bottle to lips
To soothe my tum... - Rub belly with hand
That's the life... – Raise knee and slap

Little Bunny Foo Foo

Little Bunny Foo Foo,
Running through the undergrowth,
Picking up the field mice and bashing them on the head.

Down came the Good Fairy and said "Little bunny Foo Foo, I don't like your attitude, picking up the field mice and bashing them on the head.
I'll give you 3 chances, and if you don't behave, I will turn you into a goon!"

Little Bunny Foo Foo,
Running through the undergrowth,
Picking up the field mice and bashing them on the head.

Down came the Good Fairy and said "Little bunny Foo Foo, I don't like your attitude, picking up the field mice and bashing them on the head.
I'll give you 2 more chances, and if you don't behave, I will turn you into a goon!"

Little Bunny Foo Foo,
Running through the undergrowth,
Picking up the field mice and bashing them on the head.

Down came the Good Fairy and said "Little
bunny Foo Foo, I don't like your attitude,
picking up the field mice and bashing them on
the head.
I'll give you 1 more chance, and if you don't
behave, I will turn you into a goon!"

Little Bunny Foo Foo,
Running through the undergrowth,
Picking up the field mice and bashing them on
the head.

Down came the Good Fairy and said "Little
bunny Foo Foo, I don't like your attitude,
picking up the field mice and bashing them on
the head.
I gave you 3 chances, now you've done it"
POOF!
She turned him in to a Goon.

The moral of this story is:
Hare today Goon tomorrow.

Found a Peanut

(To the tune of Clementine)

Found a peanut, found a peanut, found a peanut just now.
Just now I found a peanut, found a peanut just now.

Continue in the same manner with:
It was rotten…
Ate it anyway…
Got sick then…
Called the doctor…
Had surgery…
Died anyway…
Went to heaven…
Kicked an angel…
Went the other way…
Found a peanut…
What harm could it do…

Quartermasters Store

There were mice, mice, eating all the rice
In the stores, in the stores
There were mice, mice eating all the rice
In the Quartermaster's stores

Chorus
My eyes are dim I cannot see
I have not brought my specs with me
I have not brought my specs with me

Now fill in with your selection of verses from
below or make some up for the occasion:

Gravy gravy, enough to sink the navy
Cheese cheese, that brought you to your knees
Soup soup, supposed to feed the group
Chip chips, as big as battleships
Rats rats, as big as alley cats
Bread bread, as hard as Alan's head
Skip skip, looking a bit of a drip
Scouts scouts, chewing on some sprouts
Snakes, Snakes, as big as garden rakes
Beans, beans, as big as submarines
Cakes, cake that no one knows who bakes
Eggs, eggs, with scaly chicken legs
Goats, goats, eating all the oats
Bees, bees, with little knobby knees.
Owls, owls, shredding paper towels.

Apes, apes, eating all the grapes.
Turtles, turtles, wearing Girl Guides girdles
Bears, bears, with curlers in its hair
Foxes, foxes, stuffed in little boxes
Coke, cokes, enough to make you choke
Flies, flies, swarming 'round the pies
Fishes, fishes, washing all the dishes
Moths, moths, eating through the cloths

The Animal Fair

We went to the animal fair, the birds and the
beasts were there,
The big baboon by the light of the moon was
combing his auburn hair.
The monkey, he got drunk, and fell on the
elephant's trunk,
The elephant sneezed and fell on his knees,
And that was the end of the monkey, monkey
monkey, monkey....

Perform this in a round with other sections
repeating monkey, monkey, monkey...

Worms

Nobody loves me, everybody hates me
I'm going out to eat worms
Long thin slimy ones
Short, fat, furry ones
Gooey, gooey, gooey, gooey worms
Now the long thin slimy ones
Slip down easily
The short fat furry one stick
And when the short fat furry ones stick between
your teeth
That's when the juice goes (Make slurping
noise)

Bite their heads off
Cut their tails off
Throw their skins away
Nobody knows how I survive
On a hundred worms a day
Olay!

Oh you'll never get to Heaven

Oh you'll never get to Heaven, in a rocking chair.
'Cause the Lord don't allow, no lazybones there

chorus
I Ain't gonna grieve, I ain't gonna grieve
I Ain't gonna grieve my Lord no more

…in [name of person]'s car, 'cause [name of person]'s car, won't get that far
…in [name of person]'s boat, 'cause [name of person]'s boat, won't even float
…on water skis, 'cause the Lord don't allow, no hairy knees
…on roller skates, 'cause you'll roll right past those pearly gates
…in a limousine, 'cause the Lord don't sell no gasoline
…on a motor bike, 'cause you'll get halfway, then you'll have to hike
…in a jumbo jet, 'cause the Lord ain't built no runways yet
…in [name of person]'s pants, 'cause [name of person]'s pants are full of ants
…in a girl guides bra, 'cause a girl guides bra won't stretch that far
…on a cub scouts knee, 'cause a cub scouts knee's too knobbly

If you get to heaven, before I do, then dig a hole, and pull me through

That's all there is, there ain't no more. Saint Peter said, as he closed the door.

My Uncle

(Tune: My Bonnie Lies Over the Ocean)

My uncle fell into a pothole
In a glacier while climbing an Alp.
He's still there after 50 long winters,
And all you can see is his scalp.

Chorus
Bring back, bring back,
O bring back my uncle to me, to me.
Bring back, bring back,
O bring back my uncle to me, to me.

My uncle was proud of his whiskers,
To shave them would give him the blues.
They hung all the way to his ankles,
And he used them for shining his shoes.

Chorus

My uncle had faith in a sailboat
He had built from an old hollow tree.
My uncle set sail for Australia,
Now my uncle lies under the sea.

Chorus

My uncle made friends with hyenas,
He gave them a ride on his raft.

When a crocodile reached up and grabbed him,
The hyenas just sat there and laughed.

Chorus

My uncle annoyed his dear parents
They tossed him right off of the bus.
And if we don't mend our behaviour,
Why that's what will happen to us.

Chorus

This Little Scouting Light

This little Scouting light of mine, I'm gonna let it shine.
I'm gonna let it shine, I'm gonna let it shine
Let it shine all the time, let it shine.

All around the neighbourhood, I'm gonna let it shine. . . .
Hide it under a bushel-NO!- I'm gonna let it shine. . . .
Don't you try to blow it out, I'm gonna let it shine. . . .
All around this world of ours, I'm gonna let it shine. . . .

There Was an Old Woman

There was an old lady, who swallowed a fly.
I don't know why she swallowed that fly.
Perhaps she'll die.

There was an old lady, who swallowed a spider,
Who wriggled and jiggled and tickled inside her.
She swallowed the spider to catch the fly.
I don't know why she swallowed that fly.
Perhaps she'll die.

There was an old lady who swallowed a bird.
How absurd to swallow a bird.
She swallowed the bird to catch the spider
Who wriggled and jiggled and tickled inside her.
She swallowed the spider to catch the fly.
I don't know why she swallowed that fly.
Perhaps she'll die.

There was an old lady who swallowed a cat.
Imagine that to swallow a cat.
She swallowed the cat to catch the bird.
She swallowed the bird to catch the spider
Who wriggled and jiggled and tickled inside her.
She swallowed the spider to catch the fly.
I don't know why she swallowed that fly.
Perhaps she'll die.

dog...What a hog!

goat...Just opened her throat
cow...I don't know how
horse...She's dead of course

Banana Dance

Bananas of the world, unite! (place arms over head)
Peel banana, peel, peel banana (x2 whilst pretending to peel a banana)

Then add the following verses in and repeat the previous verses:
Chop banana…
Mash banana…
Eat banana…
Throw banana…

Tom The Toad

(Tune: Oh, Christmas Tree)

Oh Tom the Toad, Oh Tom the Toad
Why did you jump into the road?
Oh Tom the Toad, Oh Tom the Toad
Why did you jump into the road?
You were so big and green and fat
But now you're small and red and flat.

Oh Sue the Skunk, Oh Sue the Skunk
Why do you make my tires go thunk?
Oh Sue the Skunk, Oh Sue the Skunk
Why do you make my tires go thunk?
You did not look from East to West
Now on the road there's such a mess.

Oh Sue the Skunk, Oh Sue the Skunk
Why do you make my tires go thunk?
Oh Sam the Snake, Oh Sam the Snake
Why do you lie out there and bake?
You did not see that truck go by
Now you look like a butterfly.

Oh Sam the Snake, Oh Sam the Snake
Why do you lie out there and bake?
A ten-ton truck ran up your snout!
Why do you lie there stone-cold dead?
Oh Swallow Sam, Oh Swallow Sam,
What turned your body into jam?

Oh Swallow Sam, Oh Swallow Sam,
What turned your body into jam?
In the air you'd quickly speed,
An eighteen-wheeler made you bleed.
Oh Swallow Sam, Oh Swallow Sam,
What turned your body into jam?

Arm'dillo Tex, Arm'dillo Tex,
Why are you looking so perplexed?
Across the yellow line you strayed,
The truck hit you - like a grenade!
Arm'dillo Tex, Arm'dillo Tex,
Why are you looking so perplexed?

Oh Doggie Spot, Oh Doggie Spot,
Upon the road you're such a blot.
Out in the lane you boldly went,
Now your bod's not worth a cent!
Oh Doggie Spot, Oh Doggie Spot,
Upon the road you 're such a blot.

Oh Bunny Ben, Oh Bunny Ben,
Why is your body flat and thin?
Out on the road you quickly jumped,
You didn't count on getting bumped.
Oh Bunny Ben, Oh Bunny Ben,
Why is your body flat and thin?

Oh Billy Bat, Oh Billy Bat,

Why are you lying still like that?
Along the road you swooped and flapped,
But a trucker's windshield got you zapped!
Oh Billy Bat, Oh Billy Bat,
Why are you lying still like that?

Oh Turtle Ted, Oh turtle Ted,
Your shell's all broken - so's your head.
In the road you thought you'd travel,
Now you're ground into the gravel.
Oh Turtle Ted, Oh turtle Ted,
Your shell's all broken - so's your head.

Oh Possum Pete, Oh Possum Pete
There's nothing left but hair and feet
Oh Possum Pete, Oh Possum Pete
There's nothing left but hair and feet
You thought you'd beat that bus across
Now you look like a pile of moss.

The Tree Toad

(Tune: Auld Lang Syne)

A tree toad loved a fair she toad
That lived up in a tree;
She was a fair three-toed tree toad
But a two-toed toad was he.
The two-toed tree toad tried to win
The she toad's friendly nod;
For the two-toed tree toad loved the ground
That the three-toed tree toad trod.
Now three-toed tree toads have no care
For two-toed tree toad love,
But the two-toed tree toad fain would share
A tree home up above.
In vain the two-toed tree toad tried;
He couldn't please her whim.
In her tree toad bower with veto power,
The she toad vetoed him!

Boom Chicka Boom

I says a-boom-chick-a-boom! (Group copies)
I says a-boom-chick-a-boom! (Group copies)
I says a-boom-chick-a-rock-a-chick-a-rock-a-
chick-a-boom! (Group copies)
Uh-huh! (Group copies)
Oh Yeah! (Group copies)
This time! (Group copies)
We sing! (Group copies)
HIGHER!
Each time a leader adds a different variation
such as: LOWER,
WHISPER, LOUDER, TONGUE-IN-CHEEK,
SEXY, GROOVY (COOL).

My name is Joe

Hello, My name is Joe, and I work in a butter factory.
One day, my boss said to me, "Are you busy Joe?"
So I said "No".
So my boss said to me, "Can you stir this butter for me with your left hand?"
So I said "O.K."

Hello, My name is Joe, and I work in a butter factory.
One day, my boss said to me, "Are you busy Joe?"
So I said "No".
So my boss said to me, "Can you stir this butter for me with your right hand?"
So I said "O.K."

Hello, My name is Joe, and I work in a butter factory.
One day, my boss said to me, "Are you busy Joe?"
So I said "No".
So my boss said to me, "Can you stir this butter for me with your left foot?"
So I said "O.K."

Hello, My name is Joe, and I work in a butter factory.

One day, my boss said to me, "Are you busy Joe?"

So I said "No".

So my boss said to me, "Can you stir this butter for me with your right hand?"

So I said "O.K."

Hello, My name is Joe, and I work in a butter factory.

One day, my boss said to me, "Are you busy Joe?"

So I said "No".

So my boss said to me, "Can you stir this butter for me with your head?"

So I said "O.K."

Hello, My name is Joe, and I work in a butter factory.

One day, my boss said to me, "Are you busy Joe?"

So I said "YES I AM!"

Everywhere We Go-o

(Sing each line and group repeats)

Start singing lightly and increase volume every
time song repeated until a final scream through
the song

Everywhere we go-o
People always ask me
Who we are
And where we come from
And we always tell them
We're from Rothwell
Mighty, mighty Rothwell
And if they can't hear us
We shout a little louder.

Eventually finish with…

And if they can't hear us
They must be DEAF!

Always a good song if there are multiple groups
round the campfire competing.

Grand old Duke of York

The grand old duke of York
He had ten thousand men
He marched them up to the top of the hill
And he marched them down again
And when they were up they were up
And when they were down they were down
And when they were only half way up
They were neither up nor down!

(Stand up for up, sit down for down and stand
half way up for half way)

There's a Hole in My Bucket

There's a hole in my bucket, dear Liza, dear
Liza
There's a hole in my bucket, dear Liza, a hole.

Well fix it, dear Henry, dear Henry, dear Henry
Well fix it, dear Henry, fix it.

With what shall fix it…
With a cork…

But the cork is too big…
Well cut it…

With what shall I cut it…
With an axe…

But the axe is too blunt…
Then sharpen the axe…

With what shall I sharpen it…
With a stone…

The stone is too dry…
Then wet it

With what shall I wet it…
With water…

In what shall I fetch it…
With a bucket…

But there's a hole in my bucket…

There ain't no flies on us

There ain't no flies on us!
There ain't no flies on us!
There may be flies on some of you guys
But there ain't no flies on us!

Performed best with other groups throwing it
back and forth getting louder each time.

Bungalow

Leader: Hey [camper]
Camper: Hey what?
Leader: Hey [camper]
Camper: Hey what?
Leader: Let me see you bungalow, let me see your bungalow!

Camper:
My hands are high (raises arms)
My feet are low (touches toes)
And this is how i bungalow! (Performs a funny dance)

Everyone: (while copying camper's dance)
Bungalow, Bung-Bung-alow
Bungalow, Bung-bung-alow

The song continues with the person who showed of their "bungalow" choosing the next person, and so on.

Yogi Bear

(To tune of camptown races)

I've got a friend that you all know,
Yogi, Yogi.
I've got a friend that you all know,
Yogi, Yogi Bear.
Yogi, Yogi Bear, Yogi, Yogi Bear.
I've got a friend that you all know,
Yogi, Yogi Bear.

Yogi has a little friend,
Boo-boo, Boo-boo.
Yogi has a little friend,
Boo-boo, Boo-boo Bear.
Boo-boo, Boo-boo Bear, Boo-boo, Boo-boo
Bear.
Yogi has a little friend,
Boo-boo, Boo-boo Bear.

Yogi has a girlfriend too,
Cindy, Cindy.
Yogi has a girlfriend too,
Cindy, Cindy Bear.
Cindy, Cindy Bear, Cindy, Cindy Bear.
Yogi has a girlfriend too,
Cindy, Cindy Bear.

Yogi has an enemy,
Ranger, Ranger.

Yogi has an enemy
Ranger, Ranger Smith.
Ranger, Ranger Smith, Ranger, Ranger Smith.
Yogi has an enemy,
Ranger, Ranger Smith.

They all live in Jellystone Park,
Jellystone, Jellystone.
They all live in Jellystone Park
Jelly, Jelly, Jellystone Park
Jelly, Jelly, Jellystone Park, Jelly Jelly,
Jellystone Park.
They all live in Jellystone Park,
Jelly, Jellystone Park.

She'll Be Coming Round the Mountain

She'll be coming 'round the mountain when she comes. (Toot Toot!)
She'll be coming 'round the mountain when she comes. (Toot Toot!)
She'll be coming 'round the mountain, coming 'round the mountain, coming 'round the mountain when she comes. (Toot Toot!)

She'll be driving six white horses when she comes. (Whoa back!)

She'll be firing silver pistols when she comes (bang bang!

She'll be wearing pink pajamas when she comes (wolf whistle)

Oh, we'll all go out to meet her when she comes. (Hi babe!)

Cecil the Caterpillar

This one is spoken not sung, in a silly voice by someone doing lots of gesticulation.

Cecil is a caterpillar.
Cecil is my friend.
The last time I saw Cecil, he was this big. (use fingers to show average-sized caterpillar)
I said "Cecil"
He said "What?"
I said "What you been doin'?"
He said "I ate a cabbage"

Cecil is a caterpillar.
Cecil is my friend.
The last time I saw Cecil, he was this big. (use fingers to show big-sized caterpillar)
I said "Cecil"
He said "What?"
I said "What you been doin'?"
He said "I ate my Sister!"
"Cecil! You naughty caterpillar!"

Cecil is a caterpillar.
Cecil is my friend.
The last time I saw Cecil, he was this big. (use fingers to show huge-sized caterpillar)
I said "Cecil"
He said "What?"

I said "What you been doin'?"
He said "I ate my Mum"
"Cecil! You naughty caterpillar!"

Cecil is a caterpillar.
Cecil is my friend.
The last time I saw Cecil, he was this big. (use fingers to show massive-sized caterpillar)
I said "Cecil"
He said "What?"
I said "What you been doin'?"
He said "I my Dad"
"Cecil! You naughty caterpillar!"

Cecil is a caterpillar.
Cecil is my friend.
The last time I saw Cecil, he was this big. (use fingers to show average-sized caterpillar again)
I said "Cecil"
He said "What?"
I said "What you been doin'?"
He said "I was sick!"

Singing in the Rain

I'm singing in the rain, just singing in the rain.
What a glorious feeling, we're happy again.
Thumbs up! [Group echoes and sticks thumbs up.]
A-choo-cha-cha, A-choo-cha-cha, A-choo-cha-cha-cha

Add each of the following in turn as well as the previous with all the actions:

Elbows in
Knees bent
Toes together
Bums out
Chest out
Chin down
Tongue out

Woodpecker's song

(To the tune of "Dixie")

I had my finger in a woodpecker's hole,
And the woodpecker said, "God bless my soul,
Take it out. take it out, take it out, remove it"

So I removed my finger from the woodpecker's
hole,
And the woodpecker said, "God bless my soul,
Put it back, put it back, put it back, replace it"

So I replaced my finger in the woodpecker's
hole,
And the woodpecker said, "God bless my soul,
Turn it round, turn it round, turn it round,
revolve it"

So I revolved my finger in the woodpecker's
hole,
And the woodpecker said, "God bless my soul,
The other way, the other way, the other way,
return it"

So I returned my finger in the woodpecker's
hole,
And the woodpecker said, "God bless my soul
Pull it out, pull it out, pull it out, Remove it.

So I removed my finger from the woodpecker's hole,
And the woodpecker said, "God bless my soul,
Take a sniff, take a sniff, take a sniff,
Revolting!"

Coca Cola

[tune feara jacqua]

Coca Cola, Coca Cola
Makes you burp, Makes you burp.
Have another bottle, have another bottle.
Burp Burp Burp, Burp Burp Burp.

Sing in a round as per other songs.

Farmyard Carols

Split your audience into 4 groups. Each group gets a farmyard sound. (Moo, Baa, Quack, Oink)

You point at a group when you want them to 'sing' and get them to do a farm yard version of various songs.
Good ones include nursery rhymes like Twinkle twinkle, little star or Baa baa blacksheep.

Old MacDonald had a Farm

Old MacDonald had a farm, e-i-e-i-oh!
And on that farm he had a cow, e-i-e-i-oh!
There were tall cows, short cows, short cows,
tall cows,
Fat cows, thin cows, thin cows, fat cows,
Old MacDonald had a farm, e-i-e-i-oh!
(Perform actions of tall short, fat and thin)

For other verses add in the next animal into the
verse above so that you eventually have many
animals in the last verse:
Pigs
Sheep
Ducks
Eventually a duck billed platypus

Wee wee tot

When I was a wee-wee tot
They took me from my wee-wee cot
They put me on my wee-wee pot
To see if I would wee or not

When they found out I would not,
They took me from my wee wee pot.
They put me on back in my wee wee cot,
And then I gave it all I got.

When I was a Cub Scout in my prime,
I used to wee wee all the time,
Now I'm a Scouter going grey,
I only wee wee once a day.

Oggie oggie oggie, oi oi oi

You: Oggie oggie oggie!
Group: Oi oi oi!
You: Oggie oggie oggie!
Group: Oi oi oi!
You: Oggie!
Group: Oi!
You: Oggie!
Group: Oi!
You: Oggie oggie oggie!
Group: Oi oi oi!

You can also have someone primed to shout at the end:

Zigga zagga, zigga zagga, shut your mouth!
(However, don't do that if you think anyone might be offended)

Victorious (One bottle of beer)

Victorious, victorious,
One bottle of beer between the four of us,
Glory be to god that there ain't no more of us,
'Cause one of us would drink the bloomin' lot.
Amen, start again.

Victorious, victorious,
One bottle of beer between the four of us,
Glory be to god that there ain't no more of us,
'Cause one of us would drink the bloomin' lot.
Bottle 'n all, Amen, start again.

Victorious, victorious,
One bottle of beer between the four of us,
Glory be to god that there ain't no more of us,
'Cause one of us would drink the bloomin' lot.
Bottle 'n all, Cork 'n all, Amen, start again.

Victorious, victorious,
One bottle of beer between the four of us,
Glory be to god that there ain't no more of us,
'Cause one of us would drink the bloomin' lot.
Bottle 'n all, Cork 'n all. Label 'n all, Amen,
start again.

BP spirit

(To tune of He's got the whole world in His hands)

I've got the BP spirit, in my head,
I've got the BP spirit, in my head,
I've got the BP spirit, in my head,
I've got the spirit in my head.

I've got the BP spirit, in my heart,
I've got the BP spirit, in my heart,
I've got the BP spirit, in my heart,
I've got the spirit in my heart.

I've got the BP spirit, in my toes,
I've got the BP spirit, in my toes,
I've got the BP spirit, in my toes,
I've got the BP spirit in my toes.

I've got the BP spirit, all over me,
I've got the BP spirit, all over me,
I've got the BP spirit, all over me,
I've got the spirit all over me,
All over me to stay.

Kum Ba Yah (Come with Me)

Kum ba yah, my Lord, Kum ba yah.
Kum ba yah, my Lord, Kum ba yah.
Kum ba yah, my Lord, Kum ba yah.
Oh Lord, Kum ba yah.

Repeat using the following verses as desired:

Someone's crying, my Lord, Kum ba yah.

Someone's singing, my Lord, Kum ba yah.

Someone's praying, my Lord, Kum ba yah.

Someone's sleeping, my Lord, Kum ba yah.

Someone's laughing, my Lord, Kum ba yah.

Someone's Scouting, my Lord, Kum ba yah.

Someone's camping, my Lord, Kum ba yah.

Children playing, my Lord, Kum ba yah.

We are happy, my Lord, Kum ba yah.

Finish with 1st verse again:

Kum ba yah, my Lord, Kum ba yah.

Kum ba yah, my Lord, Kum ba yah.
Kum ba yah, my Lord, Kum ba yah.
Oh Lord, Kum ba yah.

Actions if desired are:

"Kum Ba Yah" hand over hand, then hands out.
"Lord" - point upward.
Other actions are as expected, for example:
"Scouting" (Scout sign); "camping" (made tent
shape with hands) etc…

Printed in Great Britain
by Amazon

72381932R00037